MONEY
POWER
For
Singles

By Tama McAleese
Certified Financial Planner

THE CAREER PRESS
180 FIFTH AVE.
PO BOX 34
HAWTHORNE, NJ 07507
1-800-CAREER-1
201-427-0229 (OUTSIDE U.S.)
FAX: 201-427-2037

ISBN 1-56414-048-2, $6.95

To order by mail, please include price as noted above, $2.50 handling per order, plus $1.00 for each book ordered. Send to: Career Press, 180 Fifth Ave., PO Box 34, Hawthorne, NJ 07507. Or call Toll-Free 1-800-CAREER-1 to order using your VISA or Mastercard or for information on all books available from The Career Press.

IMPORTANT: While much careful thought and depth of research have been devoted to the writing of this book, all content is to be viewed as general information only and should not be construed as actual legal, accounting or financial advice of a personal nature.

The ideas, suggestions and general concepts are subject to Federal, state and local laws and statutes. The ever-changing economic, political and international environment may well demand re-interpretation of some or all of the concepts presented herein.

The reader is urged to consult competent legal, accounting and tax advisors regarding all legal and personal financial decisions. This book is not meant to be utilized as a substitute for their advice.

Library of Congress Cataloging-in-Publication Data

McAleese, Tama
    Money power for singles / by Tama McAleese.
    p.   cm.
    Includes index.
    ISBN 1-56414-048-2 : $6.95
    1. Single people--Finance, Personal.   I. Title.
HG179.M374   1992
332.024'0652--dc20   92-42046
                                                                    CIP

Table of Contents

MONEY POWER
For Singles

MONEY POWER For Singles

Alone At Last.
Now What?

Many years ago, in the small village of Sher, there lived a very wise old man. How old was he? So old that the most ancient villager couldn't remember when he hadn't been their spiritual leader. And for as long as any of them could remember, he had brought them good fortune.

But as generations passed, the old sage retreated to the mountains. The villagers saw him less and less. Eventually, a band of young rebels proclaimed that the village no longer needed the sage. They hoped to assume his leadership role... and his power.

One night, a coup was secretly plotted. The plan was to trap the old man in a game of wits and show he was no longer a great leader.

The youths' leader proclaimed that an important problem had developed, that the welfare of the town was at stake. The sage had to be consulted. That night, the entire town gathered, and the old man made his trek down the mountain to meet with them.

As everyone sat quietly, the rebel leader stepped forward, his hands cupped over his head. "I am holding a white bird in my hands," he announced. "Is it alive or dead?"

What a clever trap! If the old man said the bird was alive, the youth intended to crush it in his grasp. And if he said the bird was dead, the boy would let it fly. Either way, the youth would have his sign that the old sage was no longer the infallible source of truth.

The old man spoke: "The choice is up to you, my son." Then he turned and started back up the mountain.

It's your choice!

Eat your carrots; pick up your toys; look both ways; be home by midnight; get good grades. All your life you've lived by the rules of significant others—your parents or a spouse. Suddenly, you're alone. *You*'re in charge. The choice of how you lead your newly independent life is totally in your hands.

Luckily, you're *not* alone! **MONEY POWER For Singles** will set your feet firmly on solid financial ground, help you develop self-reliance by utilizing sound money management principles, and stay by your side as you navigate your own path to financial success.

If you are reading this book to assist a friend, a loved one or a colleague adjusting to a new lifestyle of self-dependence, you will learn supportive strategies.

If *you* are the one suddenly on your own, you will learn to resist the temptation of those offering you freedom from managing your own financial life. You will undoubtedly receive offers of assistance from both vested interests and well-meaning incompetents. Either category can damage your financial future.

No one knows more about your money than you do. *No one* will watch over it as carefully as you will. And *no one* will care about its well-being as much as you.

You had better watch your own money. Otherwise, someone else will gladly work it for you—at their profit and, most likely, at your expense.

Though you will probably never win the lottery, you will likely earn enough money to sustain you for a lifetime if it is wisely managed. Some weeks may seem like two steps forward and a giant leap backward. But your financial independence will grow and with your new money skills you will take longer steps forward and smaller (and fewer) in reverse.

For the "suddenly" single

There are no medals for most martyrs. If you are "suddenly" single—through divorce or death—you have a different row to hoe than college students confronting the real world for the first time. Take charge, walk with your head high, and tackle decisions and opportunities. Striking out directionless or subtly sabotaging your progress will only inhibit your efforts. Empowerment is comforting, and financial empower- ment will also change other areas of your life in a positive manner.

Self-reliance will be your best friend, your strength to build a secure lifestyle and to move on to a new stage to play a new role.

For every single

For all of us, taking charge of our financial lives is a fundamental need and a goal you *can* accomplish with this book.

Whether you lack sound money skills because you've had a parent or spouse taking care of you, the skills you must learn are the same. And **MONEY POWER For Singles** is the book that will teach you every one of them.

Chapters 1 - 11 are for every single out there, covering the basics of budgeting, investing and interest, credit cards, insurance, financial planning (both short- and long-term), retirement planning, estate planning and dealing with a home.

Chapters 12 and 13 are particularly for those made single by death or divorce, discussing the specific problems—fin- ancial and emotional—they face and the specific solutions they should embrace.

Chapter 1

Searching For Solid Ground: Make A Budget

Assessing your income needs (what expenses must be paid on a monthly basis) and incoming funds (net monthly take-home pay) is vital to planning and implementing a budget. Unless you first determine your cash flow, you could quickly find your finances out of control. This will force you to turn to credit; but, as the federal government has proven, *no one* can spend more than they make for very long.

The beauty of a budget

A budget assists you in setting priorities and creating a financial highway so you can travel more successfully toward your goals.

The first step is to complete a goal-setting worksheet that will help you think through your financial priorities. Try to list both short- and long-term goals. Short-term goals stretch from now through the next two or three years. Long-term financial objectives are generally three years away or longer.

Engaging in this exercise might very well represent the first time that you've really thought about your finances.

So take your time and think through your priorities before committing to them.

Then, using the forms and instructions provided, figure your cash flow and net worth. In the next chapter, we'll use these figures to do some initial planning.

GOALS, OBJECTIVES & ATTITUDES WORKSHEET

Date: _____

List all your objectives under the following major categories—the more specific the better:

Retirement: (At what age would you like to retire? Where do you want to live? What leisure activities will you pursue?)

_____

_____

_____

_____

_____

Career Goals: (What job do you want to be doing a year from now? Two years? Five years? What are the things about work that satisfy you most—money, title, security?)

_____

_____

_____

_____

_____

_____

_____

Family Plans: (Marriage? Children?)

_____

_____

_____

_____

Education Objectives:

_____

_____

_____

_____

Current Income Needs: (What are your expenses?)

_____

_____

_____

Other: (Business pursuits or any other "special dreams" not covered in any of the above categories)

_____

_____

_____

_____

HOW TO SUCCESSFULLY DEVELOP A WORKING MONTHLY BUDGET

1. Calculate monthly expenses for all listed categories on the Monthly Cash Flow Statement.

2. Estimate variable expenses such as utilities, clothing, medical bills and maintenance.

3. Divide occasional bills such as taxes and insurance premiums into monthly payments on the budget.

4. Multiply weekly expenses such as food and gasoline by 4.3 to calculate monthly expenses.

5. Develop a strategy for accumulating Christmas funds *before* the holidays.

6. Don't include income taxes unless you receive a very large IRS refund each year. In that case, reduce over-payments by increasing exemptions and saving the money yourself.

7. Review all categories to reduce outgoing expenses (e.g., auto, homeowner, and other insurance, entertainment, vacations, miscellaneous).

8. Total all expenses and list in the "Total Expenses" space.

9. Calculate only dependable take-home income; do not include unreliable overtime.

10. List all net income in the space "Net Take-Home Income."

11. Subtract expenses from income. Divide that in half.

HOW TO SUCCESSFULLY DEVELOP
A WORKING MONTHLY BUDGET

12. List all credit card balances, the monthly payments, annual percentage interest (monthly interest multiplied by 12) and annual card fees. Isolate the credit card with the highest interest rate.

13. Deposit 50% of the extra budget money from item 11 into a savings vehicle such as a credit union or savings account to "pay yourself first."

14. Target the credit card with the highest interest rate and apply the other 50% to this debt. Pay only monthly minimums on all others. The total balances owed to each don't matter—what you're paying of each borrowed dollar *does*.

15. Do not become so debt-conscious that you forget to save your emergency ("rainy day") money. It's as important as getting out of debt.

16. When you retire the highest cost credit card, start on the next highest interest rate card. Again, pay only monthly minimums on the others until all credit cards have been retired.

17. When you are completely credit card debt-free, utilize OPM (other people's money). Choose one card, charge only what you can pay off within the grace period (generally 25-30 days), and pay off the balance in full each month.

MONTHLY CASH FLOW STATEMENT

Monthly Take-Home Pay: _____

Monthly Expenses: _____

Remaining Money (Take-Home Pay
Minus Expenses):   ═══════════════

Monthly Expense Detail

Savings and Investments: _____

> Include company pension plans, individual retirement plans (IRA's, Keogh's, etc.), establishing an emergency fund and general investment accounts.

Housing Costs
Monthly Mortgage Payment/Rent :   _____
Property Taxes (per month):   _____
Property Insurance(per month):   _____
Home Equity Loan Payments: _____

Consumer Debt
Dept. Store Accounts: _____
Credit Card Accounts: _____
Bank Loans: _____
Car Payment(s):   _____
Other Time Payments: _____

Other Monthly Expenses
*Auto Insurance: _____
*Car Maintenance: _____

*Child Support/Alimony: _____
*Clothing: _____
*Entertainment: _____
*Gasoline/Diesel: _____
*Groceries: _____
*Health Insurance: _____
*Household Items: _____
*Life Insurance: _____
*Medical/Dental: _____
*Miscellaneous: _____
*Organization Dues: _____
*Other Insurance: _____
*School Supplies: _____
*School Tuition: _____
*Student Loan or Tuition: _____
*Subscriptions: _____
*Telephone: _____
*Utilities: _____
*Vacation: _____

Total: _____

Present Lump Sum Obligations

Mortgage Balance: _____
College Tuition: _____
Credit Card Accounts: _____
Bank Loans: _____
Other Time Payments/Debts: _____
Total: _____

What Are You Worth?

Liquid Assets

Cash/liquid money: $_____

Checking accounts: $_____

Credit union: $_____

Savings accounts: $_____

Savings bonds: $_____

Money market funds: $_____

Life insurance cash values: $_____

Total Liquid Assets (a): $_____

Investment Assets

Stocks: $_____

Bonds: $_____

Mutual funds: $_____

Certificates of deposit: $_____

Basic company pension: $_____

IRAs: $_____

401k, 403b, TDA, TSA plans: $_____

Other: $_____

Total Investment Assets (b): $_____

Personal Assets

Vacation home or land: $_____

Rental property: $_____

Jewelry/art/antiques: $_____

Collections: $_____

Other: $_____

Total Personal Assets (c): $_____

Total Assets (a + b + c) $_____

Liabilities

Credit card balances: $_____

Mortgage: $_____

Car loans: $_____

Time/personal loans: $_____

Education loans: $_____

Home equity loans: $_____

Life insurance loans: $_____

Other debts: $_____

Total Liabilities: $_____

Your Net Worth

Total Assets: $_____

Minus Total Liabilities: $_____

Your Personal Net Worth: $_____

Additional Living Assets*

Fair market value of home: _____

Current value of auto(s): _____

Market price of personal belongings: _____

Other: _____

*Do not include these in previous net worth statement unless you plan to sell a bedroom or car to pay for three meals a day!

Chapter 2

Your New Financial Plan

Your budget is an invaluable tool for reaching your financial goals. While it might seem like creating a budget takes a lot of time, I guarantee it will *save* you time in the long run.

Arrange a system for handling money and make certain that other family members (if you are not living alone) understand the system. Then, once you have the day-to-day money matters worked out through a budget, start thinking about a more long-term financial plan. Here are some basic guidelines for establishing a financial plan that will work.

No voodoo economics

Make your spending and savings plan suit your own income, needs and wishes. Do *not* try to keep up with others. They may seem financially better off, but they might actually be deeply in debt—in poor overall financial shape underneath that facade of opulence. The status game is dangerous, the financial equivalent of Russian Roulette.

Spend your money on those things that mean the most to your welfare and happiness, not unimportant items that mean the least to you.

Plan for the entire year, rather than week to week, so you can track progress toward your longer-range goals.

Include all your dependable income and expected expenses. Don't use optimistic numbers or try to create a better-looking financial picture than reality dictates.

Plan to pay yourself first by saving at least 10% of your income. If you can't manage 10% right away, save a smaller amount on a regular basis. If you fail to stick to your budget at the beginning, don't give up. Stay with it. You will succeed if you are determined and persistent.

Review your spending and savings plan once a month. Make up your mind to stay with it, but don't be afraid to alter it if you see that it's either unreasonable or can be improved.

Where you are now along the road to financial success is not nearly as important as in which direction you are proceeding. Significant progress may take some time, especially if you have drunk deeply at the credit card well. Look for positive and regular signs of fiscal improvement.

Money Mistakes You Will Be Tempted To Make

Depending on others

The message you will hear again and again through all my books: don't depend on others for your financial future if that means losing control of basic investment decisions and the responsibility for working your own money.

Government programs, even supposedly sacrosanct ones like Social Security, can be changed with the stroke of a pen. And that wonderful retirement plan can disappear if your company does.

Not taking charge of your own assets

Most people don't learn the basics—compound interest, the time value of money, the meaning of "opportunity cost," etc. "Renting" your investments—funneling your money through financial middlemen—will severely depress your returns. Own your own investments—such as mutual funds —ones you can buy directly.

Living today, paying tomorrow

It's the dream credit card companies have been laying on us for ages: don't worry about how or when you're going to pay it back, just spend it now! Too much debt will destroy your financial future, no matter how wonderful your plans. Cut down on your charging habits and, if necessary, "cut" the plastic itself.

Believing in "something for nothing"

All too many investors desperately want to believe the unrealistic projections about financial products they don't even understand. They seldom read the prospectus—granted, most couldn't understand it—so they wind up relying on the broker or agent's "interpretations" and promises.

Following your parents' lead

Families often pass on traditions that *do not work*. The World War II generation put their money into their home, a bank and insurance. Most of them are *not* living happily off their income on some tropical isle.

Take the time to study all the financial vehicles and routes available to you. Financial dreams do not just happen. They are well-planned for and worked for over a long period of time.

No matter where you are now, everybody can learn to use their dollars more wisely. Remember: financial opportunities may be unlimited, but your investment money certainly isn't!

Chapter 3

How To Become "Fiscally" Fit

Today's emphasis on physical fitness is a positive sign that people are taking charge of their lives. But to thoroughly enjoy healthy living, you must be fiscally, as well as physically, fit. Having money may not produce happiness, but at least it will allow you to brood in a nicer home or while driving a more expensive car.

Creating long-term fiscal health

In this chapter we will elaborate on more long-term fiscal-fitness goals. It is addressed primarily to young singles, many of whom have not yet developed bad financial habits.

The first step—and I can't emphasize this enough—is to build up an emergency fund as you eliminate unnecessary debt, to "pay yourself first" via an interest-bearing checking, savings or credit union account. It is important to build an emergency fund large enough to sustain you for three to six months if you should get sick, lose your present employment, or become disabled. If this amount is more than you can amass before starting your long-term savings goals, attempt to save at least two months' living expenses. This money must be *liquid*, that is, easily obtainable without penalties.

Investigate the best yielding bank savings account, bank money market, money market mutual fund, or credit union savings plan. There should be no risk of principal on this money. So be sure your money is backed up by the organization. Some companies today offer better-looking yields by increasing the risk to your principal without publicizing it. Watch money market mutual funds for this tendency.

Step by step, inch by inch

Defer large purchases such as a new home or a new car unless you are positive you can afford them and manage *all* the payments (not just the first few months), even if your employment or other income plans turn sour.

Develop the habit of systematic investing by initiating an automatic monthly investing plan through your company's payroll department, your credit union or your checking account. This type of savings plan is flexible and can be increased, decreased or even completely stopped if necessary. The amount you choose will be automatically deducted on the same date each month and can even be transferred directly to a mutual fund institution.

Since this money is deducted before you actually see it, you won't spend it on frivolous purchases. Small amounts of money invested wisely and consistently over a long period of time can compound miraculously. Since your long-term savings—those slated for retirement or college—*must* outpace inflation, opt for mutual funds that have growth of your principal as part, but not all, of their investment objectives.

Look for tax advantages only as a last priority. Some might enhance an already good quality investment (such as an IRA shelter or UGMA tax label for college savings) *without* reducing or limiting the original investment objective. But many tax gimmicks are sold at the expense of the quality of the investment, while others might have severe penalties or surrender charges for many years. Avoid these types of investments. You can watch your money better, receive a better long-term return, and have greater control over your investment dollars in high quality mutual funds than in most alternative investments, especially insurance products.

Stay away from life insurance sold as a college savings or retirement plan, and avoid insurance annuities, long-term retirement vehicles that don't work efficiently...even for retirement purposes. The glitzy proposal ledgers tend to hide large internal charges and expenses that cut down significantly on your real rates of returns. Stick with high quality diversified mutual funds for long-range financial goals.

If you generally receive a large IRS tax refund, develop a plan with your company's payroll department to increase your tax exemptions and, therefore, increase your take-home pay. You don't have to have a child or other dependent for each exemption you claim. Just be sure not to give yourself such a large increase that Uncle Sam penalizes you for paying too little in quarterly taxes. Put that extra "raise" to work for you during the year—work the extra money that Uncle Sam would otherwise have held for the entire year. Otherwise, you are giving an interest-free loan to your government when that money would work much better for you around the house.

It is *never* too early to start an IRA or other retirement savings plan. The longer your money has to work at a reasonable rate of return, the bigger your nest egg will be over the years and the less original paycheck dollars you will have to contribute to enjoy a comfortable retirement. Don't *ever* forget that time *is* money—the financial institutions never have; that's why they want yours.

You don't have to have an MBA in Finance to build a pot of gold at the end of your working years. Time, coupled with the higher returns you'll enjoy by cutting out financial middle-men (lending institutions and insurance companies), can do much of the work for you.

Inflation is the deadliest money killer over longer periods of time, the main reason most retirees are terrified when the Social Security check doesn't come in on the third of each month as Uncle Sam promised.

Simplify, simplify

As you become more successful and receive increases in your paycheck, don't increase your current lifestyle. Instead, invest those extra dollars and learn to live *beneath* your means.

Saving and spending are *not* conflicting goals. Saving is merely *not spending right now* so that the original investment money can compound into a much larger pot of money, *more* to spend in the future.

Remember: it's not what you make that counts, but what you *take home* and keep that matters. And it's not really what you take home but what you have left after taxes and inflation that determines purchasing power. Keep track of the real rate of inflation, and direct your investments to keep pace with the real rate of increasing costs.

Why do they call it *life* insurance?

Properly insure your life with "death" insurance if you have debts or will leave behind people who will continue to need your income. There is only one purpose for such insurance: to protect your liabilities (your debts and your income).

A college student with no bills and no family responsibilities needs little, if any, death protection, no matter how cheap the insurance agent claims it is when you are young. Utility bills will also go up over time. But you don't prepay them far into the future just because they are cheaper now. You would not purchase homeowner insurance until you moved into an apartment or a home. Keep in mind that insurance isn't a wonderful thing to own—it is a necessary evil. Shop for the cheapest way to pay for dying too soon.

Insurance companies have very large, elaborate office buildings and they reward agents well for having wonderful sales pitches for whole life and universal life policies. Getting an insurance agent to talk about cheaper term policies is like getting a Mercedes dealer to talk about used Yugos. After all, insurance company agents have personal financial goals too.

Now read that employee manual

If you are employed, get a handle on your company's health, death, disability, and vested retirement benefits and options. Use those as your basic coverage only and consider other protection (such as more death or disability income insurance). Ask your employee benefit or personnel department for more information, Don't, however, act solely on their advice in critical areas. Clerical employees rarely understand complicated benefits contracts. Well-meaning incompetents can damage your financial life as gravely as any vested interest sales vendor.

Where there's a will...

Create an estate plan by drawing up a will and a durable power of attorney for disability, a document which allows a relative or friend to manage your financial affairs if you should become disabled.

Also, investigate a living will if it is appropriate in your state. These documents allow your medical wishes to be carried out even if you are not physically able to convey them.

Review your estate plan each time your personal, financial or medical status changes. As with all other parts of your total financial plan, an estate plan provides a comfortable safety net upon which you will build more positive aspects of your life.

Don't spoil them rotten

A special word to single parents: pay yourself first, but stop buying your children. Your growing adolescents might *want* expensive designer jeans and "cool" tennis shoes, but they *need* a monthly investment plan in a good mutual fund for college or other vocational training after high school graduation. Give them what you *are,* not what you *have.*

More importantly, your young adult needs a parent who offers lots of love and a firm set of values. Give them the most valuable gifts of all—your time and your love. Those cost absolutely nothing, yet produce the best future adults.

Second wind

When you have completed all of the above, you will be in excellent fiscal shape—as long as you manage to wisely invest your savings. Pick through all information about investments and read all contracts. Remember: the bold print giveth, while the fine print can taketh away. If you consider the price of a financial education too expensive, consider the much larger cost of ignorance.

Chapter 4

Little Things
Mean A Lot

You probably heard all too many times from one of your parents, "A penny saved is a penny earned."

I've found that one of the surest signs of getting old is how often you find yourself saying the same things your parents did. In my case, I've added a bit to my parents' advice: "A penny saved is *more* than a penny earned (thanks to compound interest)."

So, before we get into anything more complicated in the wonderful world of finance, this checklist will help you make sure that your budget is not hemorrhaging due to a bunch of small, pesky leaks. This chapter also provides some good advice on closing and preventing the big leaks.

Budget Maintenance Checklist

- Shop around: Review all savings, checking and investment accounts to reduce fees.
- Don't pay bills until they are actually due. Don't wait too long, though, because you will be charged late fees.
- Drop at least one credit card to reduce your payment of annual fees.
- Reduce your withholding taxes at work and pay yourself first with the additional paycheck money by investing in a short-term savings vehicle.
- Set up an automatic investment account for retirement or college funding.

- Don't prepay low-interest loans or home mortgages until you are sure future savings needs will be met.
- Increase your current death (life) insurance coverage by the amount of the outstanding mortgage balance. Then discontinue your lender's mortgage insurance.
- Don't purchase death insurance unless you need the death benefit to provide income for someone. If you are a surviving spouse without dependents, consider dropping your current death insurance policies altogether. Your major problem is living, not dying.
- Avoid health policies that pay for every office visit and, instead, opt for major medical and catastrophic policies and increase your deductibles.
- Raise the deductibles on your homeowner and auto insurance policies, but increase the liability coverage to protect yourself against a lawsuit.
- Switch regular checking accounts to interest-bearing ones. Lenders may offer no-charge checking if you also deposit some savings. This is a good trade if you deposit only the minimum for the "free lunch."
- Cancel all brokerage accounts with annual fees unless you can really get your money's worth from trading stocks and bonds (and most of you should *not* be doing this). See my book, ***Money: How to Get it, Keep it, and Make It Grow*** for much more advice on who should be investing what and where.
- Review club and organization memberships with annual fees.
- Review all book and magazine subscriptions —are they still worth it?

- Turbocharge your return on savings by researching several lenders' rates on CDs, savings or money market accounts, and other types of interest-bearing accounts. Be sure *all* investments are backed by the FDIC (Federal Deposit Insurance Corporation) in case the institution fails.

- Do not put all your eggs (emergency or rainy day funds) into one basket (lender). Spread them out among several lenders and banking institutions in the local area.

- Do *not* purchase brokerage CDs from other parts of the country. Your best information on the solvency of a financial institution is the local gossip line. Keep your short-term money close by.

- Start a 401k or 403b (TDA) supplementary pension plan at work to reduce gross income if—*and only if*—the investment vehicles are high quality. Choose mutual fund options that bypass insurance companies. You will have plenty of people living off you at retirement without helping to support an insurance agent's family now.

- Quit smoking, I *know* it's not easy, but try, try again. You'll save cigarette money and reduce your doctor bills.

- Slowly liquidate consumer debt while contributing to your rainy day money fund.

- Switch finance company loans to lending institutions that charge lower interest rates.

- Switch personal interest loans (consumer loans) to home equity loans at fixed rates if they are lower. But be sure you can repay them. You are backing these debts up with your home.

- Switch all credit card loans to lower interest rate cards. If you pay off your balances each month, switch to cards with no annual fees. Check to be sure there is a grace period between purchases and when the interest starts to accrue. Some cards charge interest from the moment you say "Charge It!"
- Don't purchase a new car. Get a one-year-old auto and let the original owner suffer the first-year depreciation loss.
- Transfer your childrens' unusual medical expenses to *their* tax returns, if they have income.
- Review, ruthlessly, the following budget categories: vacations, entertainment, clothing, miscellaneous.

Best ways to save on insurance

If your insurance agent drives a better car or takes fancier vacations than you do, wears better clothes than you can afford, or is moving up to a more expensive home than you are paying for on a 30-year indentured servant plan, you may be paying him or her too well.

Review your insurance program and cut costs while providing good coverage where it really counts. Fundamental risk management rules should be followed:

- Insure first those potential catastrophes that you or your family could not recover from, such as death, a major illness, the loss of your home, a lawsuit, long-term disability, and nursing home care.
- Then, insure against those perils that would cause significant financial hardship, such as personal property loss or theft, property damage, auto collision and damage (unless the car is old), and short-term disability.

- Retain—and pay out of your own funds—the least damaging but pesky risks by choosing high deductibles on auto, homeowner, health and disability insurance policies.

- Avoid certain individual coverages totally, such as dread disease policies, accidental death and dismemberment, cheap accident policies, hospital indemnity, return premium insurances, and all credit card, TV or other telemarketer solicitations. Never purchase insurance through credit card companies or through your monthly credit card statements. Guaranteed issue insurances without medical underwriting are enormously expensive for the coverage provided and frequently camouflage limited benefits.

- Get level-term insurance for a growing family and reduce the amount of death benefit over time as your family becomes older. This reflects your decreasing years of financial responsibility.

Chapter 5

Number Games Everyone Can Win

Asked to describe the greatest discovery of his life, Albert Einstein is rumored to have responded: "Compound interest."

Well, it doesn't take an Einstein to figure out that the higher the rate of return (interest) you receive on your money, the faster it will grow. But how fast is "fast"? How can you predict what you will actually have at any given time? And how do you take inflation into account?

The "Rule of 72"

Fortunately, there's the Rule of 72, a quick way to estimate how fast money will double at any interest rate. Just divide the number 72 by the rate of return you are currently receiving. The resulting answer is how many years it will take to double your money.

If you want to calculate the *shrinking* effects of inflation, you can use the same approach. Again, divide the number 72 by the current rate of inflation. (Look at your own bills from one year to another, not propaganda from politicians, to determine the *real* rate of inflation.) The answer will tell you when your money will purchase only half of what it does today.

Looking at how the formula works for interest, we find:

At 3% per year, your money will double every 24 years (72/3 = 24 years).

At 6% per year, your money will double every 12 years (72/6 = 12 years).

At 8% per year, your money will double every 9 years (72/8 = 9 years).

> At 12% per year, your money will double every 6
> years (72/12 = 6 years).

Let's examine how we can use the same formula to see
inflation's effects far away on the time horizon.

> At 3% inflation per year, your money will pur-
> chase only half what it can now in 24 years
> (72/3 = 24 years).
>
> At 6% yearly inflation, your money will shrink
> to 50 percent of its current value in 12 years
> (72/6 = 12 years).
>
> At 8% inflation per year, your money will erode
> by half in 9 years (72/8 = 9 years).

It's all in the timing

Two points should be made clear by these sample cal-
culations. First, the higher the interest rate (or the rate of
inflation), the larger the account value (or the greater the
damage inflation will cause over time). More importantly,
doubling the interest rate (or the inflation factor) will *more*
than double the return (or shrink the dollar) over longer periods of time.

In other words, twice the rate of return does *not* equal
twice the result. The longer the period of time your money has
to work, the greater the gap between lower and higher accum-
ulation values. Therefore, it is vital that you seek higher
returns on your long-term money and know if the inflation
rates are climbing.

Whether or not the Einstein story cited above is true,
interest is indeed a powerful thing. Perhaps you are in your
early twenties with lots of years for your money to accumulate. You can utilize this concept the best, using time to do
much of the work for you. Just keep track of the rates of return you receive and stay ahead of inflation each year.

Perhaps, though, you are muttering to yourself that this
knowledge comes too late to keep the wolf from your door. The

concept remains the same, whether you are 25, 35, or 55. The only difference is that the less time you have, the harder your money must work. Since your time is more limited, you have no time to lose. If you do nothing, in five more years you will just be older, poorer (due to inflation), and have an even larger financial problem to solve.

If you begin now, you may fall short of your desired financial goal; if you do nothing, you are doomed to fail from the start.

Would your banker tell a lie?

Financial institutions realize that consumers have learned to shop for competitive interest rates on their savings and investment dollars. So interest rates at many lenders are more cleverly marketed today.

Bankers also realize that most customers have no idea how compounding really works. If the marketing department can confuse you through quoting interest rates on their financial products, they can trap your savings.

You can be sure of two things: no one—not your lender, not a large corporation, not your insurance company, and certainly not your government—will offer you any more for your money than they have to. We can also assume that they will attempt to charge you as much for borrowing *theirs* as possible.

Deposit $1,000 into a passbook savings account today, and you will fall asleep watching it compound.

Now *borrow* $1,000 from the same lender, and watch the interest you pay mount to 7% or more...compounded in a different manner. You work your money at 3% and they work it (by lending it out) at 7%. Considering that it may even be your very own money that you are borrowing back, that's some partnership!

When it works *for* you

Compound interest works best the more frequently the money is compounded. So let's analyze the effect of various compounding methods on a lump sum ($10,000) with an advertised rate of 5% for one year:

Simple interest	=	$500 profit
Compounded semi-annually	=	$506 profit
Compounded quarterly	=	$509 profit
Compounded monthly	=	$512 profit
Compounded daily	=	$513 profit

The more often the money is compounded, the greater the profit over a specific time period. Over longer periods of time, this relatively small difference will expand and provide a much larger nest egg for you.

When hunting for interest rates on bank financial products, always request the ***effective annual yield.*** This takes into account the various types of compounding and puts all offers on an equal basis. When borrowing money from a lending institution, ask for the ***compounded annual percentage rate***, *not* the simple interest rate.

If this sounds too complicated, there is an easier method. Just ask the account officer one question: "If I put my money into your institution for one year, how much profit will I have at the end?" Compare this answer with others and choose the institution with the best offer.

If the teller cannot give you an answer, ask to see the manager. If he or she cannot calculate an accurate response, run as fast as you can with your money out the door.

Any novice with an inexpensive compound interest calculator can figure out that answer. Do you really want to leave your valuable dollars in a place where the employees can't even calculate the compound interest they are supposed to be adding to your account?

Find an institution that pays you the respect you deserve. The lender who offers you the highest return on your money respects you the most. If the large institutions mismanage their assets, your government will find a method for you to pay for the financial mess. Who will cover any losses *you* suffer because you have mismanaged your own investments?

Chapter 6

Credit Cards: Friend Or Foe?

The most dangerous and personally destructive financial problem facing consumers today, whether they earn their living by their hands, their wits, or through investment income, is the abuse of credit. Most consumers are living beyond their current financial means.

One destructive status game is buying a home that you really can't afford to impress people you really don't like very much. (Do true friends care whether your abode is furnished in early American or early orange crate?)

Another dangerous game is paying for things you can't afford with credit cards. After all, if you can't afford something, what in the world are you doing borrowing money that must be paid off with interest!!!? Perhaps you only do this to feel wanted—you must love the calls and letters you get when you miss a credit card payment!

Take a long, hard look

Make an honest examination of *all* your debt now. This might be shocking if you've become accustomed to thinking only in terms of monthly payments rather than the actual size of the monkey on your back.

I'm not saying that you shouldn't use OPM (other people's money), but that when you do, it should be interest-free. In fact, you *can* borrow the lenders' money each month for *free* —by paying your credit balance off in full every month.

If, on the other hand, you have succumbed to the propaganda that you could live now and pay later, have it all today and pay off a little at a time, there is an effective strategy for whittling down that mountain of installment debt:

- First, list your cards, their annual fees, the total balances due, and each card's annual percentage rate. (Use the form on p. 40.)

- Highlight the card charging the highest interest rate.

- Total up your budget and subtract all monthly take-home income (excluding overtime and bonuses unless you *know* those dollars will be dependable). The remaining money is the "fat," left-over dollars that are slipping through your fingers. Recapture their value by putting half of them into a savings vehicle to "pay yourself first," and the other half directly toward the balance on the card with the highest interest rate. The size of the balances on your cards do not matter. It is the cost for the borrowed money (the interest rate) that really counts.

- Do not get so zealous with paying off debt that you forget to build your emergency fund. If you should find yourself short of cash, you will be borrowing again, putting yourself further into the debt hole. Dig yourself out slowly but systematically.

- When you have totally paid off the highest APR (annual percentage rate) credit card, tackle the next highest card and continue to pay only monthly minimums on the remaining cards. Defer *all* major purchases until your consumer debt is under control.

- Bring the entire family into this process. Have weekly family council meetings at the kitchen table. It is vital that your child(ren) understand you are no longer a "tree with money growing out of your ears." Ask your children for their suggestions to help cut down expenses. Develop a positive attitude toward everyone's progress. Offer congratulations for individual efforts.

- Develop a new attitude regarding saving and spending. Saving is simply deferred spending—working your money first through compound interest until it has grown enough to purchase those larger things you desire in the future.

Avoid the "yes, buts"

While you are doing this, you won't be living as high on the hog as you've become accustomed to. But resist the temptation to shelter your children from financial realities. This is their only chance to learn good money management skills. Otherwise, when they graduate from high school and college they will have the technical skills to make money, but no knowledge of how to effectively *manage* that money.

Have the entire family join the hunt for low-cost or free family entertainment, such as county park events, community festivals, local sporting events, biking, museum, and wildlife tours, and summer family picnics. This will, in addition to cutting living expenses, strengthen your family values and encourage greater communication.

Can't get it back

If you are wasting your money, you can get help. But if you continue to waste your time, no one can buy that precious commodity back for you. Start now. There will never be a better time, a cheaper time, or a more convenient time. Where you are now on the road to financial success is not nearly as important as in which direction you are moving.

A credit card can be a valuable tool, like a hammer to a carpenter. But it will become the most dangerous financial nightmare you will ever live through if it makes you feel richer than you really are and encourages you to spend beyond your current income. Neither countries nor households can borrow themselves into future prosperity, and too many individuals and families are being seduced into giving away their future incomes to finance current levels of over-consumption. Every credit card issued in this country should have the following warning label printed on it: **Warning! Overuse Can Be Hazardous to Your Wealth!**

Danger signals of debt

Credit is dangerous if it makes you feel richer than you really are, causes you to spend more than you make, or encourages you to live beyond your current financial means.

The following danger signals must be addressed immediately. Do not let time pass without actively turning around your spending habits. Things don't get better over time. In fact, they tend to become worse. Look for warning signs such as these:

- You don't know how much total debt you owe (just the size of the payments), and you're afraid to add it all up. Perhaps you even hide monthly statements from your family;
- You pay only minimum monthly payments—or less—each month;
- You have reached your credit limits on some cards and are more actively borrowing with others to make up the cash difference;
- You borrow for purchases you used to buy with cash. (Remember real money?);
- The portion of your income used to pay debts is rising, and you no longer contribute to a savings or investment account. You have little or no emergency fund savings;
- You are often late paying some of your bills, and you juggle the budget to keep up. This month's credit balances are even larger than they were *last* month;

- You have borrowed money to pay for regular household expenses such as rent, food, clothing, gas or insurance. You borrowed more money to pay off an overdue debt or have just consolidated loans. Now you're applying for additional credit cards to borrow even *more* money;

- You are currently drawing from savings to pay regular bills and have little or no rainy day money left—you don't have enough savings for at least three months' living expenses if you are laid off, disabled or become ill;

- Your liquid assets (savings) total less than your short-term debt, and you often use a cash advance from one credit card to make payments on others. You are paying regular bills with money earmarked for other obligations. More than 18% of your after-tax income goes toward consumer installment debt;

- Creditors are sending overdue notices. You postdate checks so payments won't bounce, then hurry to the bank on payday to cover checks already written. Checks are bouncing on a more frequent basis;

- Life without credit seems unthinkable.

If any of the above describe your current financial health, you are a prime candidate for credit card management strategies. Sit down tonight and put together a simple but complete budget. My book, **Get Rich Slow**, now available in a brand-new second edition, has a simple budget that can help. Post your budget on the refrigerator as a reminder of your new commitment to financial freedom. Don't yield to procrastination.

CREDIT CARD COMPARISON SHEET

Issuer	Amount Owed	(APR)	Annual Fee	Minimum Payment

Chapter 7

Getting The Credit You Deserve

Despite the woes cited in the previous chapter, I am not against credit cards, just their misuse. Credit cards can be helpful as planning tools and may indeed be absolutely necessary as the first step in establishing a credit history.

While credit is all too easy to get for many Americans—who soon find themselves teetering under a huge weight of debt—single people can have trouble establishing credit or obtaining even the most fundamental credit. Those suddenly single through divorce or the death of a spouse might find themselves for the first time unable to qualify for the credit they might need to purchase a new home, a car, even a new outfit. Young people setting up their own residences and just starting their careers will not have an employment history they can take to the bank.

May I see your card, please?

In our society, even those who are not in the habit of using credit can find it difficult to get along without a credit history.

Getting a credit card under your own name—without relying on a spouse's income on your application—can be the first step in developing a credit history.

You will want to obtain one or more bank credit cards. While they might be easier to obtain, department store cards do not carry the same clout in consumer credit ratings.

Find the best card for your money

The first step is to research the comparative rates and terms available from various banks, using the checklist at the end of this chapter. All credit cards are *not* created equal. Visa and MasterCard credit cards are offered through individual banking contracts, with each institution setting its own set of qualifications and rules—interest rates, how interest is calculated, terms of cash advances, annual fees, etc. If you are turned down at one institution, try another. They may be more generous with their qualifications and find you more appealing as a customer.

Hunt for credit card offers in newspapers and magazines. Some banks will offer cards with no initial annual fees and advertise very low interest charges. Examine the offers carefully for notices of hidden expenses such as no grace period between the purchase date and when interest starts, annual fees at a later date, a mandatory cash advance, or other agreements in the fine print.

If you continually have difficulty qualifying for a credit card, try to obtain a collateralized card. These look like the "real thing" but require not a promise to pay, but a deposit (the collateral) which they place into an interest-bearing checking account. The issuer will give you a line of credit (a card) up to the amount of money you have deposited with them. If you have no other alternative, collateralized cards can provide that credit history you need to become a good credit prospect in the future.

Don't give up too easily or too early

If you're turned down for a credit card, be assertive. Personally visit the local lender, request to be treated on an equal basis with any other type of customer who may apply, and be persistent.

If you are repeatedly denied and feel you have been discriminated against, continue your fight for credit. Tell the card company you will, if necessary, go to the media with your story. Document all telephone conversations, the names of people you speak to, and copies of all written letters you send. If necessary, bring documentation of all assets to a local lending institution with your request. Finding a sympathetic ear in a woman banker, if you are a divorced female for example, might help your cause.

After all, you are not asking for the moon, just a small credit line of, say, $250. Offer to remove any savings or other banking business you do with the institution if they reject you. Tell them if they can't trust you, you certainly cannot trust them enough to continue doing business with them. Remember your friends, and remember your enemies.

Your credit card shopping list

When comparison-shopping for credit cards, keep the following questions in mind:

1. What is the annual fee? The annual percentage rate?
2. Does the card have a fixed interest rate or a variable one that will go up when general interest rates increase?
3. How long is the grace period (the number of free days after purchase) before interest charges start? (Some low-interest cards have _no_ grace period. Watch for and avoid those.)
4. Is there a charge for late payments?
5. Are there transaction fees for purchases or for cash advances? For over-the-limit purchases?
6. What is the annual percentage rate for cash advances? Is it higher than the cost of money for regular purchases?
7. How soon does interest start after you receive a cash advance?
8. Have you read ALL the fine print?
9. Do you understand every promise?
10. Will this new card encourage you to feel richer and spend beyond your means?

Chapter 8

Investing: The Myths, The Truths, The Ways

For someone who has to get a handle on the financial world for the first time, there is a tendency to create or latch onto myths in an attempt to get rid of some of the awful confusion. Here are some of the most popular myths:

Myth #1: **Put your money in the hands of a financial expert or a large financial institution. They have the reputation and the know-how.**

This myth exists largely because institutions spend billions of dollars annually to create the illusions of credibility, to give their representatives titles which may camouflage their lack of real credentials, and to convince you they are primarily concerned with your financial welfare when, in truth, they are focused on a single purpose: to sell, sell, SELL.

Their job is not to provide you with objective and competent investment advice but to get your signature on the bottom line of one of their investment applications.

Your responsibility is to look beyond the sizzle of the sales pitch to ferret out the real meat of any potential investment vehicle.

Myth #2: **Tax savings should be a primary thrust of your financial strategy.**

"Tax-deferred," "tax-deductible" and "tax-exempt" are wildly successful marketing phrases used to direct billions of dollars into the coffers of insurance companies, state projects and municipalities, and onto brokerage ledgers. They can also be sugar-coatings to hide mediocre or inferior investment vehicles.

The reason such gimmicks work is that many investors will do almost anything to save taxes. They will make poor financial decisions in the light of more important goals such as the flexibility or direct control of their investment dollars. They will limit access to their money and incur severe penalties. They will ignore the necessity of outpacing inflation. They will unknowingly do all of the above...just to avoid the tax man.

Consumers, instead, should consider the following investment priorities, in this order:

(1) *the purpose for the investment* (an emergency fund, purchasing a home, funding college, saving for retirement, planning a business);

(2) *the ideal and optimum investment vehicle* (money market mutual funds, conservative mutual funds for long-term money, or bank CDs);

(3) finally, any *tax advantages* which will enhance the above criteria and make the investment perform even better (IRA, 401k, 403b, SEP, UGMA or KEOGH).

The quality of the investment vehicle is more important than *any* tax advantages. If you must give up something, give back the tax gimmick before sacrificing the quality of the underlying investment.

Myth #3: You have more important things to do than look out for your investments. You should let a financial institution do that for you.

Although you have probably fought in the jungle of the work world to make those investment dollars, you will be told that the world of money is so dangerous and complicated that you should not manage it by yourself.

The fact is, you have nothing more important to do with your time than learn the truth, not the hype, about what to do with your money, and then to do it.

Myth #4: **Some get-rich-quick schemes really work.**

In fact, some schemes *do* work—just not for *you*. They work for the people that *sell* them.

Whether it's a dirt-pile gold scheme out West, a limited partnership that must be bought today, or a newsletter money guru who, for a small price, will tell you how to become a millionaire, the only proven method of accumulating wealth is the old-fashioned way: working hard for it and then carefully diversifying into investments you can understand and control.

The truths of investing

As I've pointed out these myths, I feel obliged to serve up the most reliable truths:

- All investments go up and down, including those with insurance companies and banking institutions. Most small investors do the wrong thing at the wrong time. So diversification is *always* the best investment strategy.

- Savings accounts and CDs alone will *not* make you rich because they will *not* outpace inflation.

- Bulls (investors who believe the stock market is going up) make money and so do the bears (those who fear the stock market will fall). But the piggies (those who invest out of greed) wind up with nothing. Remove all the animals from your investment planning and money management and you'll have a lot less manure to wade through.

- No one knows the future, not even money gurus who try to convince you otherwise. Markets usually overreact. So never invest when driven by greed or fear. Investment performance relies on p-r-o-f-i-t-s at the end of the fiscal year, not on p-r-o-p-h-e-t-s beforehand.

Some basic investing principles

Although the stock market might change direction every five minutes, basic investing rules haven't changed in the past 50 years. Here are some reminders that may help calm your fears and provide you with some basic directions:

Always buy quality. Don't look around for potential bargains, purchase on the advice of others, or attempt to find companies that can make you rich quickly if they will just turn around or make that breakthrough.

Never invest out of greed. The small investor is noted for buying in at the top and selling at the first sign of uncertainty. He is also usually wrong!

Invest for the long term. Develop a long-term strategy and stick with it. Chasing after profits by jumping from one investment vehicle to another will simply leave you tired, disillusioned and poorer.

Diversify, diversify, diversify. Put your eggs into a wide variety of baskets. If you invest in 90 companies, but they all produce oil or dining room furniture, you have not managed your risk well. There is a correlation between similar companies which may move downward together.

You cannot eliminate risk. But you can *manage* it through diversification and sound investment principles. If you keep all your money in a bank, eventually you might go broke—"safely." You certainly are aware of what might happen if you put all your money into the stock market. And even bonds go up and down in value.

Short-term money should be guaranteed. Emergency funds for short-term goals must be guaranteed (by someone) or pose little risk of investment principal. Goals within a three-year time horizon can be put into money market mutual funds, bank CDs, bank money market demand accounts, even credit unions.

Long-term money must consistently outpace inflation. Your long-term investments must have some growth potential.

Invest for comfort, not speed. An investment which can move up quickly probably can move down just as fast. Don't chase last year's "best" because this year is new and the basic economic dynamics will never be quite the same. Past performance is no guarantee of future results.

Don't micro-manage your investments. Unless you are a trader or want to be actively engaged in managing your investment portfolio, find a good mutual fund that has developed a consistent track record and keep your eye on it. Trying to second-guess markets will just add volatility to your basic strategies.

Don't shop solely for the highest interest rates or yields. Those high rates may be misleading or achieved through increased risks. There is no such thing as a "safe" 20%, 15%, or even 10%.

Short-stop money

I've spoken a great deal in this book about the advantage of investing short-term money in money market mutual funds. Here is an explanation of what those funds are and how they work.

Money market mutual funds (not money market bank accounts) are separate pools of investor dollars managed by a portfolio manager (usually an investment company). The portfolio manager purchases only short-term obligations, those usually maturing in a year or less. Interest fluctuates on a daily basis.

Money market fund investors can request check-writing privileges. This benefit offers instant access to your funds (similar to the way a checking account works).

Money market mutual funds can be researched through consumer magazines and media advertisements. They are not insured as a whole by any governmental body. And they are not all created equal. Some may offer better yields, but at higher risk to principal. It is vital that you thoroughly read any fund prospectus (your investment contract).

Stick to money market mutual funds that invest only in U.S. Government Treasury bills (short-term U.S. obligations) and U.S. Agency issues. Higher yields do not necessarily mean smarter banking.

These funds make great short-term storage pots. Until a college tuition check is needed, the money can be quietly building up. And with daily compounding, your cash is working 24 hours each day, just like the money owned by the large financial institutions.

Money market mutual funds have some limitations, though. Most request an initial deposit of at least $1,000 and have minimums for checks written, such as $100.

Since it does not take a rocket scientist to purchase government obligations, you should avoid any money market funds that have distribution fees (commissions). There should be only a small management or expense fee (under 1/2%).

Marathon money

Since, as we've discussed, the primary goal of long-term investments should be increasing your purchasing power, it is best to put this money into conservative equity income mutual funds, the "turtles" of the mutual fund family. They move slowly up and down because they are so highly diversified. They contain bank CDs, cash, blue chip stocks (avoid those which have more than 50% of their total investment in any type of stocks), corporate bonds, and U.S. government bonds.

For your retirement funding, the most serious money you will ever invest, utilize a combination of bank certificates of deposit, money market mutual funds, and conservative equity income mutual funds. If you are younger, you may want to round out your portfolio with a small amount of global (not international) mutual funds. This mix will diversify your portfolio as well as any millionaire could his or hers. Perhaps even better.

A sample investment portfolio

30% bank Certificates of Deposit

10% Money Market Mutual Funds (investing only in U.S. Treasury bills and U.S. Agency issues—with check writing privileges).

50% Equity Income Mutual Funds (If you are retiring soon or living on a fixed income, use a mix of 20% Equity Income and 30% U.S. Government note and/or Bond Mutual Funds.)

10% Global Mutual Funds (Retirees: you probably should skip this category and increase your holdings an extra 10% into bank CDs.)

Once you have positioned your investment portfolio, *leave it alone*, whether interest rates go up or down, whether the stock market crashes tomorrow, whether bond values change as interest rates move. Leaving your portfolio alone makes no money for the financial industry, which is why they encourage you to move your money often. Every time they sell you a "hot" investment product, a new commission is generated for the agent or representative, and new investment capital comes into the company that pays their commission.

If you have followed my recommendations, you have built a financial bicycle that will work well in all kinds of investment weather. You have tires that stay close to the ground and hug the road on the turns (your bank CDs); you have fenders to keep the mud from splashing you (a money market mutual fund if your lender gets into financial trouble while the FDIC bails it out); a comfortable seat (a stodgy, boring equity income mutual fund); plus some handlebars (either global mutual funds or U.S. Government mutual funds for older investors and retirees).

Chapter 9

Managing Your Money Pit

You might have inherited total ownership of a home through the death of a spouse. Perhaps you received your primary residence as part of the divorce settlement, purchased real estate as part of your investment portfolio or just desire more space, greater privacy and part of the American dream. In any case, eventually you might decide to refinance, remodel or sell your current home. (If you are presently looking for a new home, my first book, *Get Rich Slow,* now in a brand-new second edition, will give you the rules for purchasing your money pit.)

'Tis the season to be wary

Spring brings renewed signs of another growing season and good weather. Those balmy warm days might also motivate you to spring clean, remodel, paint, or repair winter damage to your home and your property. How can you be sure you will receive the greatest value for your dollar?

First and foremost, *get it in writing.* Get every promise, all specifications, dates of starting and completion, and all monetary arrangements down on paper. This avoids any later misunderstandings as to what the original terms of the contract were.

When you first sit down to discuss what you want, be sure to *be specific and very clear.* Ask the contractor to go carefully over his/her understanding of what you expect. Once a project begins, it is difficult and expensive to make changes.

Read through *and understand every word* in the contract you are asked to sign. The fine print (look on the back, too) was important enough for the company's lawyers to include. It should be as important for you to understand. If you don't understand all the words, terms or phrases used, ask questions. Don't be intimidated into feeling ignorant.

Never let a contractor start work on your premises until you have seen the ***Workman's Compensation certifications,*** a ***commercial liability insurance policy,*** a ***fidelity bond,*** and a ***state license,*** if applicable. This protects you in case of an accident so that you cannot be sued for injury to a worker on your property. Failure to request such information might ultimately be very costly to you.

Ask for references. Competent contractors will be pleased to provide the names of satisfied customers. Call these people. Ask how they found your contractor, what work he has done, and consider visiting the project, if it is in your area. You can call a county association or the city or county building depart-ment to ask about the contractor's reputation.

Offer as little up-front money as possible. Avoid paying the entire bill in full until the project is completed and you have personally inspected it or had the work inspected by someone else. Many companies receive their materials on credit and have only their labor costs at risk until a job is completed. Therefore, you will have something to bargain with if a pro-ject is not completed to your satisfaction.

Do not allow workers to enter your home when you are absent. If necessary, arrange a convenient time when you can be there. Keep your important papers, charge cards, Social Security checks, and money out of sight while strangers are working on your property.

If your project is extensive, call your county or city build-ing code department to see if a ***building permit*** has been issued to your contractor. Also, ask if there are any building practices which must be followed as you describe the work that will be done.

If you are not satisfied with the work as it progresses, con-tact the company's owner or manager *immediately* to discuss the problem. Do *not* allow work to continue without ironing out problems or misunderstandings. Workers on the site do not usually have the authority to change or alter any previous instructions. Have all changes or new agreements written either on the original contract or on a new contract signed and dated by both you and your contractor.

Get two or three estimates before deciding on a specific company or agent. Do *not* be pressured into signing through fear or greed. Special sales, one-time deals or last-chance offers should not make your mouth water. They should make you skeptical.

If you have sufficient cash, *think twice about financing* the work. A company might lead you to believe it is cheaper to finance than to spend your savings. But they might not be giving you totally objective advice—some companies make extra money from finance companies if they can convince you to finance. It is usually a better idea to pay cash than to borrow.

If you do finance the project, you might have two contracts rolled up into one: 1) an agreement to complete the work by the contractor; and 2) an agreement for payment with a separate lending institution or finance company. If any contract changes are made or the project is canceled, you must contact *both* parties, not just the contractor, to make the adjustments. When a contract is completed, you should also request a statement of payment in full on your account from the contractor *and* lending institution or financing company.

If a presentation is made at your home, *do not sign on the first appointment.* If a company is reputable and does quality work, it will not force you to sign a contract immediately. Take some time to think over the quote and compare it with others.

If you are pressured into signing a contract that you decide you do not want to honor, you might have a right to void it within 72 hours. (This applies only to contracts signed in your home, not at the company's place of business.) It is far better, though, to take your time *before* you sign anything.

If a deal sounds too good to be true, it might be. Take a few days—or longer—to compare and research. It is much easier to protect your money while it is still safely inside *your* pocket than to retrieve it from someone else's.

Remember, you do not purchase what you have been told —*you buy what the written contract states.* Blind faith and trust are no foundation for a good business relationship. You want to buy the steak, not the sizzle.

Using your home for a change

Refinancing could lower your monthly mortgage payments as well as total mortgage interest. But shopping for mortgage money in today's lending arena requires more than asking about current interest rates. You must gather the following information from several local lenders to make a competitive decision: 1) the current interest rate; 2) the points (percentage of the loan principle) required to lock in that interest rate; 3) closing costs; and 4) additional fees.

When you find a mortgage that looks good, get a written estimate of the closing costs as well as a promise of a 60-day lock-in rate. Don't be sold on any gimmicks, such as a low mortgage rate with higher points, or be lulled into a lower-than-current-market rate adjustable mortgage that will later move up much more quickly than the market. Let the lender assume the risk of rising interest rates. Insist on a fixed rate.

Comparing one mortgage offer against another is easy if you understand how points affect the ultimate interest rate. You might have been taught that one point is equal to one percent of the borrowed mortgage loan—forget that. To compare one mortgage offer against another, figure one point is approximately equal to an additional 1/8% of interest added to the stated interest rate.

For example, compare the following deal: 7.75% and two points against 8% and zero points. First, convert the points to equivalent interest, then add on the stated interest rate. Two points = 1/8% x 2 = 1/4% + the stated 7.75% = a total of 8%. So, 7.75% + two points is exactly the same as 8% + zero points.

By converting the interest rates and the points into the same terms, you can find the most competitive deal.

Whether you pay the points in up-front money or roll them over into the new refinanced loan, the math is the same because you are not giving away free up-front money. You are losing the use of that money for 15 or 20 years or even longer. That means there is a cost to you whether you pay the points out of your pocket or borrow them.

When to refinance

When should you refinance? In general, refinance when the current interest rate is 2% lower than what you are paying, or whenever you can pay a smaller monthly payment over the same period of time or the same sized-payment over a shorter period of time. If you have an adjustable mortgage today, consider refinancing to a fixed mortgage while rates are so low.

If you are currently supporting a 30-year indentured servant plan, consider shortening up the time of the loan to 15 or 20 years while maintaining the same monthly mortgage payments. In this manner, you will save thousands of dollars over the length of the mortgage!

When you have found the best combination of interest rate and points, look for the cheapest closing costs and smallest extra fees. In addition, try to negotiate for the ability to pay real estate taxes without an escrow account. In that way, you can work your own money in an interest-bearing account un-til tax time. Request an interest rate lock-in, so the numbers don't change when you sit across from your lender to sign final agreements at the closing. Don't give up a lower cost of money for these—all things being equal, the extra benefits will help you keep more dollars in your pocketbook.

Does it matter if your mortgage is sold? I am more concerned about the solvency of lenders when I am loaning them my money rather than when borrowing money from them. Check your loan agreement to be sure that if your loan is sold, it cannot be demanded earlier and the promised interest rate can't be increased.

Many people advise pre-paying mortgage principle to buy down the length of your mortgage, but this is not always a good idea. Perhaps you should be stashing those extra dollars into a college fund or a retirement plan. What good will it do to have your home paid off early if you have no college fund when you need it? How will you eat three meals a day if you retire with a paid-up house over your head but not enough retirement money for a comfortable feeling in your stomach?

Your home as a tax shelter

When you sell your home (primary residence) at a profit, Uncle Sam expects you to share the wealth on this capital gain with him. In most cases (with the exception of a one-time $125,000 exclusion granted after age 55), any gain will be currently deferred but taxed when you purchase a less expensive home or decide to rent permanently.

Therefore, it is vital to record and keep track of all improvements and eligible expenses that can add to the cost of your home. You will only be taxed on the difference between your original price *plus* improvements and the sale price minus selling expenses.

Improvements vs. maintenance

An *improvement* is a replacement or addition that increases market value, adds life to the property or creates new uses for it. It reduces gains because costs are added to the basis when the property is sold. If it is within two years before or after the sale, the profit might be added to the costs of a replacement residence to defer taxation.

Any improvement must remain with the house in order to qualify as an addition to the tax basis. The deductions allowed are: (a) materials only, if the projects are do-it-yourself; (b) rental items and "outside help" wages; and (c) related costs (i.e. shrub removal, required surveys). It is also a good idea to take "before" and "after" pictures in case you have to substantiate your claim. By all means, save any and *all* receipts ...even small items add up over the years.

Maintenance is a repair or replacement of items that provide proper functioning and prevent structure deterioration as a whole. They are *not* deductible.

Sometimes, the complete job is classified as an improvement. For example: the painting and wallpapering of a room being remodeled. Another example might be the restoration of neglected property needing a complete overhaul. The work done plus the materials are capital expenditures and the property cost basis is increased by the total of all work.

Real property vs. personal property

Real property is connected to the land, such as the house or the garage. Everything else is personal property. On occasion, personal property can become real property if permanently attached (i.e. built-in stereos and TVs).

Homes are nests to raise your family in and havens for enjoyment. They are *not* great investment vehicles. Buy only the home you can afford, and don't fall prey to the real estate industry's myths.

After age 55, if you have lived in your primary residence for three out of the last five years, you can eliminate up to $125,000 of your lifetime personal residence real estate profits.

Be careful to avoid some common pitfalls. *If* you use your exemption now and ultimately re-marry, neither you nor your new spouse will be eligible for another exemption during either of your lifetimes. So if you plan to re-marry and want to live in a home which neither of you currently owns, each of you should sell your homes *before* you marry. That way each of you can eliminate up to $125,000 profit on each property.

Chapter 10

Retirement
Ready Or Not

Years ago the government had what everyone thought would be a wonderful idea: tax workers, then use those taxes to provide a stipend to the elderly (who wouldn't live very long anyway). It seemed a sound idea at the time: the many young and healthy support the older and feebler.

Now, the government is left with a dilemma. Knowing full well that it can't provide all the money you will need at retirement, Uncle Sam also realizes that if he motivates you too much to save, growth will stagnate and recession could set in. Every politician knows that a recession is deadly to his or her career. Therefore, long-term priorities are sacrificed for political expediency.

Inquiring minds would like to know: if the government isn't working on the retirement problem, and Americans are not contributing funds to support themselves in their old age, then who is going to worry about it?

It certainly won't be America's companies, many of which are scaling back on employee retirement plans.

Promised retirement funds will come from your company pension (if it is still in business), subsidized by Social Security (if it is there for the middle class). The remainder of the retirement pot is *your* responsibility.

Retirement myths to avoid

Here are some popular myths about retirement finances and my harpooning of each:

Conservation of principal should be a retirement fund's top priority.

Absolutely not! Conservation of **purchasing power** should rank as the primary objective of any retirement plan. Inflation is the deadliest money killer over long periods of time. It's not what you make on your money that counts; it's what you make above inflation. Regardless of your age, you must achieve some growth on your investment portfolio.

Fixed income vehicles alone—CD's, government bills, notes, bonds, corporate bonds, and insurance fixed annuities —will not outpace inflation over time. Growth without undue risk should be your retirement investment objective.

What happened to my parents won't happen to me.

Folks don't actively plan to fail in later life. They simply fail to plan. The last generation put investment money primarily into the wrong places: a home, banks, and insurance policies and annuities. They were not taught what inflation would do to their savings over time or what they could accomplish if, instead, they worked their own investments. The only retirees currently financially comfortable and independent are those who watched after their money and worked for it for their own benefit, utilizing time value of money concepts while outpacing inflation.

I will need less money at retirement when living costs will decrease.

The only bills that will stop are the mortgage on your home and the excruciating college tuition you might now pay. Inflation won't stop, even though your current income and raises will (replaced by a smaller monthly pension with little or no adjusted living increase). Your dentist won't fill cavities anymore but will, instead, present you with a whole new set of teeth. Income, property, school, and other federal, state, local and user taxes will continue upward. The cost of groceries, medical prescriptions, treatments, and other services will continue to escalate.

You will live longer, perhaps even long enough to outlive your retirement nest egg. Like an older home, you will need more upkeep. A $100,000 retirement fund goal today will buy less and less in future years.

I will pay fewer taxes after retirement.

To pay for the large current bills we owe as a society, future costs of health care, and increased social benefits, the price of all levels of government will grow. If you intend to be in a lower tax bracket, you will be living on less money than you are today. Therefore, you will be in *worse* financial shape. You had better *not* be paying fewer taxes, or you will have a lifestyle *less* comfortable than you are currently enjoying.

I have Social Security and my company pension to depend on.

As discussed above, the aging of America is putting a large crimp into that plan.

It will be easier to save for retirement in a few years.

The fallacy in this mode of thinking is that future income will not be needed for college tuition, a larger home, more expensive cars, and an increased lifestyle. If you can't find the relatively small contributions today to start saving for retirement, how will you earmark even greater sums in five or ten years when additional drains on your income might leave you with even less discretionary investment income?

I'm still young, I have **plenty** *of time to save for my retirement.*

Time is money, and compound interest is the eighth wonder of the world. The more time you have to compound your retirement funds, the fewer original investment dollars will need to be saved.

Assume your goal at age 65 is to accumulate a lump sum of $100,000, and you expect to earn 10% annually on all money you invest.

If you start saving at age 25, you will need to contribute only $16 per month. Wait until 35, and you will need to contribute $44 per month. Waiting until age 45 will cost you $131 per month. If you hold off saving until age 55, you will be looking desperately around for $484 per month to invest.

By letting compound interest (over a long period of time) do most of the work, you can achieve your financial goals with less money.

I'm too old to start now.

Maybe you are no longer age 25, but if you wait longer, your goal will become that much more unreachable. You are running the most serious race of your life, whether as a volunteer ahead of the pack or as a victim pulled along by the deadly effects of inflation and increasing costs for the health care, housing, consumer products and services you will depend on as you mature. The time to start seriously saving is always *now!*

There will only be me.

Don't be too sure. Today, older children are moving back home (often with their own children) due to divorce, the death of a spouse, or as a single parent with a child. Today's grown children are also waiting longer to marry and leave home and are more likely to come back home when severe financial problems occur. In addition, you might have grandchildren and the desire to provide gifts or assist in their educational dreams.

The equity in my home is my retirement fund.

Personal real estate, as too many of you have soberly discovered, doesn't always go up. At best, it barely keeps pace with inflation. However, as home prices increase so does the cost of living. With retirement funding, you must *outpace* inflation over the long haul, not merely keep up with it.

Therefore, you will not fund your retirement based principally on your home's appreciation. When your liquid assets are consumed, how will you eat? By selling off a bedroom or a bathroom? You will need a comfortable roof over your head (that will not look so cheap if you have to buy down and purchase a smaller home to realize your hidden capital gain profits). You will also need a comfortable feeling in your stomach from eating three meals a day. You need other investments that don't depend on inflation for future benefits.

If I save everything today and then die young, I won't have fun living.

If you save 10% of your income for retirement, you have 90% left over for living purposes. If you can't live comfortably on 90% of your income today, you are over-spending and over-consuming. Saving and spending are *not* conflicting goals. Saving is merely not spending *today* so you can spend more *tomorrow.*

The $100,000+ mistake

If you are eliminating your IRA contribution for 1993 because it is not deductible from your gross income for tax purposes, you are making a major mistake. One that could cost you hundreds of thousands of dollars!

Unfortunately, Congress lets no good deal go unpunished for very long. So, for some, the tax deduction that felt so good and erased a maximum of $2,000 per worker off that W-4 has been maimed by the 1986 Tax Act. But the death of the IRA has been greatly exaggerated.

Before you throw away a silver bullet that Congress still allows, consider the following:

Suppose a taxpayer makes an annual $2,000 *totally non-deductible* IRA contribution each year as opposed to merely investing $2,000 per year in a taxable investment. Both the non-deductible IRA and the taxable investment capital are invested in the same investment vehicle averaging 10% per year.

The following is the result of each investment at the end of 20 and 30 years for a taxpayer in the 28% bracket:

At the end of:	Non-deductible IRA	Taxable Investment
20 years	$126,005	$ 84,272
30 years	$361,887	$ 189,588

The longer the period during which money can compound, the larger the gap between the IRA total and that of the taxable investment.

If any portion of the IRA account can be deducted, the advantages over time will be even *greater!*

Deposit the maximum into that IRA every year, deductible or not.

Retirement planning strategies

Any financial goal more than three years away calls for long-term strategies designed to score returns that outpace inflation. Avoid individual stocks, bonds and insurance company solutions because the risks on principal will be too great (through the lack of diversification) or they will not race well against the ravages of long-term inflation pressures.

Investing through mutual funds remains the best method of staying in charge. You will be able to watch your money (through daily newspaper reporting) and stay in control of your investment capital. Mutual funds allow you to redeem your money promptly when you want or need it. Since you are by-passing the financial industry and going straight to the investments themselves, you will likely receive a better overall return.

If your mutual fund has a better year, so do you. Perhaps the most important reason to invest in mutual funds is that they can offer you a millionaire's portfolio even if you don't have a million dollars to invest.

This means that your nest egg will be sheltered from the effects of specific market corrections.

For retirement funds, I recommend the equity income types because they are dull, boring and stodgy—but win the race against inflation. For detailed investment strategies, whatever your marital, economic or age status, get my second book, *Money: How to Get It, Keep It, and Make It Grow.*

Medicare supplements

If you think picking a winner on Derby Day is difficult, try ferreting through the fine print, risks, exclusions and limitations to find an insurance contract that will be there if you need supplemental health coverage. With more than 200 policies to choose from, Medicare, Medicaid, and Medigap coverage can be confusing, abused by some in the insurance industry, and oversold to seniors who have little knowledge in this area.

Most retirees know that Medicare Part A comes automatically with arthritis and varicose veins. Medicare Part B can, and should be, purchased via a monthly premium deducted right from your Social Security check. Above this basic hospital and physician care, Medigap insurance should fill in gaps and provide additional health benefits not covered by the Medicare system.

Comparison shopping might become easier now that policies are becoming more standardized. But abuse is rampant in this type of insurance. You must investigate potential policies as if your life depended on it. It ultimately might.

There is no centralized regulation in this area, no winged avengers to protect you from purchasing a defective product. You must use your consumer instincts to research this area carefully.

Look into it

Start your research at the library, using consumer magazines that rate various companies and their respective policies. Don't depend on endorsements from any organization, even those which focus on the elderly. They may push their own products or might have little knowledge of this tricky type of insurance coverage.

Look thoroughly into the fine print, the sections marked "Exclusions, Limitations, and Risks." Do not be guided by one insurance company rating. Remember that insurance companies *pay* most rating agencies for their own ratings.

In addition, *never* purchase death or medical insurance on a first sales presentation, especially one in your home. You are not buying encyclopedias or vacuum cleaners here. This is a very important part of your life. Search out several companies with good marks from unbiased magazines and listen to several agents' pitches. Some companies even offer insurance policies without agents attached to them. In either case, always request a specimen contract and take several days, even weeks, to look carefully through and compare one policy with another. Don't compare price. Compare benefits and value.

A picture might be worth 1,000 words, but insurance jargon takes on a life of its own. Don't assume you understand a contract. This is not the same English language you learned in high school. Terms can be very deceptive. Some companies use misleading terms to sell inferior policies because they know the public will believe generic translations for specific definitions and stated benefits.

Insurance purchase checklist

This should be a long process. Do *not* purchase before you:

1. Consider more than one policy;
2. Obtain and read a specimen policy from each company you are considering;
3. Research a company's ratings from several rating agencies;
4. Compare policy language with that in other insurance contracts;
5. Ask agents to compare their products against others you are considering; this technique can be successful—it's called "competition."

Competing agents might tell you policy problems that the other agent overlooked. You really cannot afford to trust anyone whose total livelihood depends on *selling* you something, regardless of how nicely the agent dresses, how pretty, handsome or pleasant he or she seems, or how honest his or her eyes. Even Cinderella knew she was marrying money when she dropped her slipper.

Long-term care insurance

The same caution should be utilized when purchasing nursing home and custodial care policies.

Never purchase out of fear or greed. If any agent attempts to use these tactics to induce a sale, escort them out of your neighborhood. All policies are not created equal; some are much better than others. There might be little relationship between premium costs and quality, but cheaper premiums are not necessarily better buys. There are no sales in the health care area. If a policy sounds too good to be true, it probably is.

There are too many pitfalls in long-term-care policies to note here. You must do some research in this area with publications that can help you spot gaps in coverage and show you how to get the greatest value for every premium dollar spent.

Assuming you have found the company from whom you want to purchase a policy, make sure you answer fully each and every question requested on the application. This is no time to develop amnesia or tell little "white lies." An insurance company could later void benefits to you because of a previous material misstatement.

Read over every question and look over your entire insurance application before you sign it. Be sure any blank questions or blank spaces are filled in or marked out by a line.

If an agent refuses to write some condition down in response to a medical question, insist that it be marked on the application anyway. A dishonest agent could omit serious information that might cause benefits to be denied or restrictions added. When you sign that application, you are taking full responsibility for the truthfulness of *any and all* information contained in it, whether you or the insurance agent omitted the information.

Always request a specimen policy. If the agent refuses to give you one, end of story. No one would purchase a car without first kicking the tires, and no one should purchase something as important as health coverage without first seeing the merchandise.

When you receive your insurance policy, re-read it. You have a certain amount of "free-look" time in which you can send it back to the company and receive your premium back.

The above are only general advice suggestions. The health care and long-term-care environment are constantly changing. You must do more research than this book has room to relate. Good financial consumers shop for health or nursing home insurance the same way they do for their groceries and their poultry, by comparing benefits and prices and by investigating for themselves.

Chapter 11

No, You *Can't* Take It With You

One of the biggest difficulties estate executors face is finding the necessary papers to carry out the wishes of the deceased. The result: their (*your*) best intentions might not be carried out, or certainly not in an expedient fashion.

So, don't keep saying, "One of these days, I've got to get organized," until it's too late. Do it now!

Everyone should have an organized list of assets (what you own), liabilities (what you owe), and vital papers in the event of a serious illness or death. In addition to bank account books, many material documents should be organized for safe keeping and convenience.

CD passbooks, IRA Account statements, and investment information should be neatly organized in a fireproof box. Stock certificates, U.S. Government savings bonds, and other negotiable securities should be listed and then locked up. Request that your brokerage or mutual fund company hold original certificates (SIPC covers any such losses up to $500,000 per investor) and maintain only account statements in your record file. Staple new statements together and reorganize whenever you have time.

Insurance policies should be kept among your important papers. Be sure to keep them updated each time your financial circumstances, personal life or health undergo significant change.

That rule prevails for other documents—your will, power of attorney, living will, and any trust documents. Review your total financial life once a year, including your estate plan, to see if these documents still coincide with your current wishes and objectives.

Gather all company employee benefit booklets, papers, union benefits, group insurance certificates and retirement plan statements together. Employees today have such a vast array of benefit options that some of these could slip through the cracks and away from your heirs.

Let them know about the estate *now*

Make critical pieces of information known at least to your executor and keep them within easy access. For example, if you desire to be cremated after death, don't just state it in your will—tell your children, relatives, parents, etc. Wills might not be read until later in the estate or probate process...long after you're *buried*.

Debts owed to you and ongoing contracts for products or services are a part of your net worth, and, therefore, part of your estate. Have all debts owed to you put into writing, even those owed by your children or other relatives. This protects you in case of their death and gives you legal standing as an estate creditor. Parents often loan their children money without expecting them to pay it back in the future. But you might want the loan money refunded in an estate situation.

Keep a copy of your annual tax returns. These give vital information regarding assets held on the date of death and reliable details regarding taxable income and other transactions. Make a habit of adding a copy of each year's 1040 to your estate planning files.

Let all individuals named in your will, trust, powers of attorney, or living will know they might have responsibilities. You might want other professionals such as your attorney, your doctor or your minister to have copies of these documents to reinforce your wishes. Someone should know where you hide items such as safety deposit keys.

Know your options

Investigate all estate-planning options. None of them fit everyone, and all have negative aspects. You must make good compromises, considering your unique circumstances. Never move ahead on the basis of a magazine article or a media program. View all options carefully before selecting the best course for you. Ask tough questions as you would with any potential investment. There are disadvantages to *every* estate-planning solution, including trusts. Weigh the risks and benefits of each.

Estate planning doesn't come easy to anyone. But despite resistance to begin the process, you can easily complete the worksheets on pp. 72 through 77.

The executor/administrator

If you become the executor or administrator of an estate, interview several attorneys for estimates of legal fees. Do not automatically use the attorney who drew up prior legal documents. Part of your job as a fiduciary (someone entrusted with the welfare of the estate) is to seek competent and cost-effective services. This is a new area for most folks. Take your time and ask questions throughout the process.

An executor might have duties such as listing assets, inventorying contents of safety deposit boxes, and locating the decedent's property. They might be helpful in the acute assistance of a business. Sometimes they can prepare and file estate inventories with the court and work with property in another estate.

Insurance policies should be gathered and insurance companies notified. Property and auto insurance needs might be ongoing. New arrangements must be made to keep all properties and cars insured.

Creditors should be notified, bills must be paid. When in doubt that a bill is legitimate, defer payment until it can be researched. There might be conferences with attorneys, insurance agents, accountants, appraisers and/or insurance adjusters. Do not become so overwhelmed that you make poor decisions. Let no one pressure you into significant action or force you to make hasty decisions. If necessary, discuss such matters with professionals or trusted companions.

Government insurance claims such as Social Security, disability benefits or veterans benefits might be due or need to be stopped. The post office must be directed as to how to handle a decedent's mail. Banks will be contacted, and income checks should be cashed, returned or appropriately filed. There is always paperwork such as waivers, property transfers, insurance policy changes, and changes of ownership on certain assets.

You have responsibilities to the estate's beneficiaries, perhaps to yourself, and to other interested parties. Do not make any permanent investments at this time. Use only storage pots such as bank accounts at FDIC lenders or money markets. You can get a financial education later, then begin to look at other investments.

Insurance companies fail, stocks go down, bonds default, and salespeople occasionally take advantage of ignorance and naivete. You must constantly remind yourself of the prudent disposition of the money under your care.

As much as possible, put professionals between you and your new responsibilities. Make them accountable for basic directions and legal advice. This will protect you against potential future liabilities.

Insist on being informed throughout the process and request ongoing bills for services rendered. Do not wait until the estate has been closed to request a total accounting of all fees. Federal and state estate planning laws, estate taxes, income taxes and general estate planning ramifications are too complex to be effectively dealt with here. Use experts but keep yourself in charge of basic decisions. Expect objectivity and competence in all your dealings. Do not be shut out of the process. If you are a surviving spouse, this is your life. Ask how you can assist to maintain costs and move things forward as quickly as possible.

Estate Organizer

Important Names/Phone Numbers

Relatives: _____

_____

_____

Employer: _____

Attorney(s): _____

_____

Insurance Agent(s): _____

_____

_____

_____

Financial Planner: _____

_____

Accountant: _____

_____

Other: _____

_____

_____

_____

_____

Doctor's Names & Addresses

Doctor (s): _____

_____

_____

_____

_____

Dentist: _____

_____

Location of Personal Papers

Will: _____

Power of Attorney: _____

Trust(s): _____

_____

Birth/Baptismal Certificate: _____

Marriage Certificate: _____

Military Records: _____

_____

Social Security Card/No.: _____

Other: _____

_____

_____

Investments (Portfolio Planning Worksheet, pp. 76-77)

Bank Assets (Portfolio Planning Worksheet, p. 76-77)

Real Estate (Portfolio Planning Worksheet, p. 76-77)

Credit Cards (see Credit Card Record Worksheet, p. 40)

Insurance Policies (company & location)

Property: _____

_____

_____

Auto: _____

Death (Life): _____

_____

Health: _____

_____

Disability: _____

Medigap Health: _____

Long Term Care: _____

Commercial: _____

_____

_____

_____

_____

Location of Titles

Primary residence: _____

Rental real estate: _____

_____

_____

Car(s): _____

_____

_____

Mortgage: _____

Title insurance: _____

Property deed: _____

Safety deposit box location: _____

_____

Income tax returns location: _____

_____

Any other papers or documents: _____

_____

_____

_____

_____

_____

PORTFOLIO PLANNING WORKSHEET

Primary Investment Objective:_____

1. Cash, Checking Accounts, Emergency Funds, CDs

Where Deposited	Objective	$ Value	Percent of Portfolio
_____	_____	_____	_____
_____	_____	_____	_____
_____	_____	_____	_____
_____	_____	_____	_____
_____	_____	_____	_____
_____	_____	_____	_____
_____	_____	_____	_____
_____	_____	_____	_____

TOTAL   _____   __100.00%__

2. Retirement Programs, College Funding, Vehicles For Other Goals:

Name of Vehicle	Objective	$ Value	Percent of Portfolio
_____	_____	_____	_____
_____	_____	_____	_____
_____	_____	_____	_____

_____	_____	_____	_____
_____	_____	_____	_____
_____	_____	_____	_____
_____	_____	_____	_____
_____	_____	_____	_____
_____	_____	_____	_____
_____	_____	_____	_____

3. Regular Investment Programs (IRA, SEP, 401K, TDA, profit-sharing, ESOP, savings bonds):

Name of Vehicle	Amount of Investment	Frequency	Present Value
_____	_____	_____	_____
_____	_____	_____	_____
_____	_____	_____	_____
_____	_____	_____	_____
_____	_____	_____	_____
_____	_____	_____	_____
_____	_____	_____	_____
_____	_____	_____	_____
_____	_____	_____	_____

Chapter 12

Facing Divorce
Or Death

The term "suddenly single" refers to a life change brought about when a "significant other" is no longer in your life. There are two major causes for sudden singlehood in modern America—divorce and death.

The faces of divorce

First, let's take a look at the financial ramifications of divorce, which are often complicated by legal considerations and, usually most importantly, emotional turmoil.

Attorneys will assist you only with the legal considerations (unless of course you're female and the attorney is *L.A. Law*'s Arnold Becker).

Although legal considerations might seem overwhelming and tend to overshadow less immediate factors, the financial consequences of divorce will be long-lasting, possibly permanent. If little thought has been given to the disposition of assets, both parties can come away with the short end of the financial stick.

For instance, the wrong person might get the house in a divorce QDRO (settlement agreement) and need to sell it quickly because there is not enough income to maintain the dwelling.

Therefore, in negotiating any divorce settlement, the parties must consider both *hard* dollars and *soft* dollars. Real estate values are considered soft dollars because the actual fair market value can vary so widely and fluctuate so much over time.

However, while the house's current market value is being bandied about like a pawn, no thought might be given to the fact that the future owner will pay real estate commissions and closing costs, and perhaps even capital gains before netting a profit on the sale of the asset.

The wife usually receives the home in divorce settlements, often with little thought as to whether she will be financially able to maintain it. Of what value is this kind of settlement if you need income, yet cannot sell off a room to feed your children or pay rising taxes, school levies or maintenance costs?

Securing the pension piggy bank

Another asset that must be given a great deal of attention during a divorce negotiation is the pension of one or both spouses. Although state laws vary, generally the couple will share those benefits accrued during the life of the marriage. If the employer's plan allows, pensions can be divided in several ways. What if the worker dies before retirement age? What if the worker elects not to retire? What if the worker quits or for some other reason does not collect retirement benefits at all?

These risks can be hedged or at least reduced. One method is to purchase a term insurance policy on the life of the worker for the future value of the retirement benefits. The spouse can act as owner and also be named the beneficiary. The worker—the insured—usually pays the premium.

If the policy lapses for non-payment of premium, the spouse has the right to continue premiums and, as owner of the insurance policy, can exercise all control over the contract.

Disability risks can be reduced through the purchase of a waiver-of-premium rider on the above term insurance policy if the worker is insurable. This ensures that if the worker becomes disabled, the policy can continue in force without more premium payments.

Always purchase term insurance rather than more expensive whole life, universal life and other such types of polices since the benefit is needed only until retirement age.

There is absolutely no need for a cash value when it cannot be used anyhow.

If there is an insurance policy already in force that can be utilized to reduce this risk, the spouse can be added as a collateral or irrevocable beneficiary (one which can't be removed by the worker without the spouse's permission).

More important than wealth

Health benefits can be another great concern during divorce proceedings. If the spouse was carried on the work-er's health insurance group plan, he or she can continue his or her insurance for a period under COBRA (Continuation of Benefits Reform Act), though he or she will now be respon-sible for the payments previously made by the employer.

If you are healthy, you have the option of looking around for a less expensive carrier. If you are sick, you probably will not be accepted by another insurer.

Health-care benefits for children, of course, can also be a major concern. Fortunately, many companies allow workers to continue health coverage for minor children after a divorce. Be sure benefits are secured either by collateral assignment or by company authorization to garnish a salary if necessary to keep them flowing.

Insurance is also important in ensuring that child-support payments will be made even if the breadwinner meets an untimely demise. In fact, most divorce decrees state that the major breadwinner must maintain a life insurance policy at least until the children are 18 years of age.

ERISA (Employee Retirement Income Security Act, a set of complicated government regulations that provide some protection benefits for divorced couples and their children) may also offer some help. You may not always know all the answers, but you must know enough to ask: (1) what am I entitled to? and (2) how can I apply?

Complications

All of these issues, as well as such considerations as the tax consequences of alimony—tax-deductible by the payer and taxable to the recipient—mean that working out a final agreement may be difficult.

Since there is always a risk of not getting payments in the future, I favor taking as many assets *right now,* in cold hard cash lump sums or close substitutes. Even if future payments would be greater, the risk always exists that these promised payments, for one reason or another, might stop. A bird in hand is usually safer than one overhead.

Social insecurity

A divorced spouse might have the same right as a married spouse to Social Security benefits. Even if the insured worker (ex-spouse) has remarried, the divorced spouse should investigate this option.

Ordinarily, a divorced spouse loses Social Security rights when he or she remarries. But benefits may continue without any reduction for a widow or widower who remarries after age 60 or for a disabled widow or widower who remarries after age 50.

When a worker starts collecting retirement or disability payments, the divorced spouse may receive benefits if: (1) he or she is age 62 or older; (2) he or she does not qualify for benefits that equal or exceed one-half of the worker's full amount; and (3) the divorced spouse was married to the worker for at least ten years.

Consult your Social Security office for details, as changes in the law continually affect benefit provisions. Discuss your individual circumstances (and request the English translation of the jargon you just read).

A divorce checklist

Here are some other matters that you should not overlook when going through the emotional trauma of a divorce:

- If you receive stocks or bonds as part of a divorce settlement, unique tax consequences apply. When you sell the stock (since there was no tax on the transfer at the time of the divorce), you will pay the full difference between the original purchase price and the fair market value at the time of the sale. In other words, you will owe taxes on all of your profits *from the date your ex-spouse purchased it,* not from the date you received it as a settlement asset.

• Creditors usually are satisfied at the time of the divorce. If a new one surfaces and expects payment from you, contact your attorney. Even if you have been indemnified by the settlement agreement, you may need legal counsel.

• Credit ratings can suffer in a messy divorce. Rebuild credit as soon as possible. A good employment record, consistent income, and good savings and checking habits are signs that you can handle credit, though your past history may indicate otherwise. Place 100 words in each credit report from the major credit rating services explaining clearly why payments were delayed and how you can now maintain a constant income flow to manage your credit card debt.

• Change all insurance policies to reflect your current beneficiary wishes and all employer group death and retirement plans. Ask the personnel or benefits department to see original application or beneficiary change forms so you can be sure any changes have been processed.

• If you are reassuming your maiden name, go through all important documents like your Social Security card, retirement plan accounts, other employer group benefits, individual insurance (life, health or disability) policies, and keep all documented changes or insurance policy endorsements.

• Get advice on how to file next year's 1040. If you have dependent children, you will get a better shake by claiming "head of household" status than "single with children."

• Be sure you have severed all ties with your former spouse—safety deposit boxes, car titles, or titles of other personal property.

• Have your personal belongings insured separately under your own homeowner insurance policy. Reassess your auto insurance as you may now qualify for better rates as a single person than you did as married. Your sex, age and a good driving record may help.

• Be sure you have current and proper titles to all property you now own, including that transferred during the divorce settlement.

• Take a videotape (or camera snapshots) of all your personal property for insurance purposes. This is also a good time to have those special antiques or pieces of jewelry appraised for their current value.

A widows & widowers checklist

• If you've inherited stocks, bonds or other investments, don't make changes *at least* until you have read this book. Too many vendors use this vulnerable opportunity to sell financial products. When making lasting financial decisions, you should have a clear head.

• If you have received individual stocks or bonds, you might want to keep a few. If they seem risky, or if you have limited assets, liquidate them. Then add these hard dollars to your short-term CDs. If you don't need the money, you can keep them and pass them to your heirs who will not have to pay taxes on the profits.

• If you have a few bills, own your own home, and are more concerned about living than dying, why do you need to own insurance? You may need those dollars for daily living. Perhaps your estate will satisfy your bills after your death. If, however, you are still responsible for raising children, you might need a bundle of cheap term insurance.

- Check on spousal benefit options such as ERISA or COBRA health benefits, company pension plans and Social Security benefits. Apply immediately; processing takes time. In the meantime, you will use your own dollars instead of those you may qualify for. If you shop for health or disability insurance, compare "apples-to-apples." Request specimen contracts and ask several agents to compete. Ask each agent to compare the contracts of other companies you are considering.

- Transfer your property deed and car title(s) to your name. Request several death certificates from the funeral director to collect various death benefits. Understand the various forms of ownership for savings accounts, CDs, securities and real estate. Each has benefits and disadvantages. Consider the best compromises given your unique circumstances.

- Contact the benefits departments of the following: (1) the employer; (2) Social Security; (3) any insurance companies for which payment receipts have been discovered among personal papers and belongings. Sometimes even a small receipt of a premium payment will trigger a death benefit from a source which might be otherwise overlooked.

- Notify banks, postal authorities, and others who may have a general power of appointment or a remainder interest in the estate of the deceased (anyone who may want to know and has a legal

right to notification by mail or by personal
telephone contact).

* Tend to pressing bills. At the time of a death, all
creditors want their money because the estate
may be wrapped up or the money in the estate
may not be sufficient to pay all debts. Do not be
pushed into paying bills until you know they are
valid, and until you have been able to ascertain
what must be paid now and what can be put off.

Chapter 13

Moving On
With Your Life

If you are suddenly single because of the death of a spouse, placing a loved one in a nursing home or a divorce, you must first gather support in the personal areas of your life. Then, you must ready yourself to do what you might never have done before—take care of the finances.

Reading this, you've probably conjured up an image of a housewife who has never worked and never had to balance a checkbook. But that's just a stereotype. I know many men who would be accused of forgery if they endorsed their pay-checks—their wives have taken care of the finances throughout the marriage.

I assure you, no matter who you are or how you came to be suddenly single, if you are physically and mentally fit, you can manage and direct your own financial affairs.

Returning to the womb is impossible; retreating under your bed covers until the new millenium impractical. Resist such urges, no matter how attractive they may seem at the time.

Be yourself and plan your personal steps slowly. Here are some suggestions from my single clients to help along the way:

- **Blame someone else** for everything bad that has happened. Government bureaucrats have fine-tuned this technique into an art form. It can work for you, too.
- **Watch soap operas**—by comparison, your life will look like the proverbial bed of roses.

- **Start a new hobby.** Wonderful therapy and, you never know, you might just start a collection worth money.

- **Be yourself** and let yourself cry if that's what's necessary. Don't feel you have to "put on a happy face" for friends or family. If you're grieving, go ahead and grieve for awhile.

- **Keep your grown children at bay.** Don't move in with them and don't let them move in with you to "protect you." This will only stifle the independence you're going to need to feel and develop. As one of my clients ruely noted: a woman can raise six children, but six children can't take care of one mother.

Take a deep breath and ...

When you feel emotionally ready to face such matters, you must formulate a budget to assess what income is available for living purposes and continue paying regular household bills, being careful to live frugally, at least until you determine exactly where you are financially.

Concentrate on today and the ordinary financial tasks, even if you don't feel motivated. You can let the dust pile up but not those monthly bills. Take a day-to-day approach to other duties, but do *not* avoid the basics outlined here.

I never knew it cost so much to stay alive!

Continue to pay regular living expenses—the mortgage or rent, utilities, credit card payments and car payments—even if you don't feel like concentrating on money matters. Force yourself by scheduling bill-paying sessions once a week. Your credit rating is at stake here. Most creditors care more about their account ledgers than about your personal problems.

Don't use plastic solutions for psychological short-term fulfillment. Loading up on credit cards will present you only with more serious financial problems later.

Halt all current checking and credit card programs you can without penalty, and get to someone (an accountant, a good friend, a consumer credit counseling agency) who will teach you some basic checking account management if you have no experience in the matter.

Don't be too afraid to seek help. It is vital to find answers now and to maintain continuity as much as possible. Cut down on unnecessary paperwork and consolidate checking or savings accounts. Frequently, spouses have individual filing or checking procedures, sometimes even separate financial lives. You may have inherited an incomprehensible system of money management.

Call several institutions and check on their current rates for savings passbooks, interest-bearing checking accounts, money market demand accounts or senior citizen specials. Then pool your dollars into a few areas: one savings account or a money market that offers instant liquidity (instant access to your money), and one checking account (preferably one that offers daily interest).

Keep most of your funds liquid because living alone might require extra cash. ***Don't buy any investments now!*** This includes bonds, tax-free mutual funds, insurance policies, insurance annuities, municipal (tax-free) bonds, and, particularly, limited partnerships. None of these are appropriate short-term investments.

Stay away from financial salespeople. If you act hastily, you could make an irrevocable investment decision that will lock up your money and subject you to serious penalties for withdrawals. You might even choose a vehicle you can't change at all—ever!

You cannot afford to trust anyone right now, especially someone whose commission and welfare rely on your purchasing their product.

Unless you have inherited millions (in which case you are probably not reading this book but are on the phone to several financial planners whose loyalty you can purchase at hourly rates), you can manage your financial affairs better and more carefully yourself.

Concentrate on getting through each week and on building your financial knowledge. In the meantime, you can get all the flexibility you need from your checking or savings account and a money market mutual fund.

Begin boning up on finance, but stay away from public seminars and the advice of insurance agents, stockbrokers, financial advisors, bank trust or estate planning departments. These all represent vested interests. Pigs will fly before you will receive objective financial advice from such sources.

Don't be so concerned with the yield on your short-term money that you forget about bank solvency. The duration is too short to worry about losing a few dollars in interest as compared with the general safety of the institution.

It must be in here somewhere

Gather all important-looking papers (including homeowner and auto insurance declarations, utility bills, car payment books and the original sales agreements, company benefits booklets, etc.) on the kitchen table and sort through them. Buy inexpensive file folders and set up a separate slot for each category. Getting financial areas organized will provide a sense of accomplishment and a sense of greater control over your life.

Purchase a large desk calendar with big blank spaces and record all incoming monthly money (paychecks, Social Security checks, insurance pension payments, or other regular benefits you can depend on) with a green marker. Mark all outgoing regular bills (general monthly expenses) in red. You can plan as far ahead as one month, but if this time period seems overwhelming just plan one or two weeks at a time.

After you have subtracted the bills from your income, arrange other debts in order of their importance. Organize which ones (or portions of ones) you will pay and when. Always leave yourself with a slush fund to handle financial surprises.

This organizational system will demand less real thinking as well as save time. Check your desk calendar each week to see which bills must be paid and when. Write out those checks and move on to more positive and more pleasant activities.

One step at a time

Until you feel more confident about handling your finances, do not take on any major financial commitments, debts, or make any long-term financial decisions. Don't co-sign or lend any of your new assets to relatives and/or children. You might need them back later, and the promised repayments may not materialize.

Don't think that $100,000 or $150,000 in hand makes you rich. Stay employed or consider re-training for a career you would enjoy. This is healthful physically and mentally and will get you back into the mainstream and out of isolation. Some spouses have been secured behind the walls of home-making for so many years that they are terrified to start a new lifestyle. Get career counseling and find positive friends.

Take credit

Get your own personal credit if you don't already have a significant credit history. Women and self-employed workers might have a more difficult time getting institutions to accept them as customers in this area. So be persistent, and don't become discouraged if one lender turns you down. Charge occasionally so you can develop a working history of using your credit card.

Think of your new credit card as a convenience and emergency card only and as documentation to other lenders you may want to impress in the future. Don't charge anything so large you cannot pay it off during the ensuing grace period. And be sure that the card you choose *has* a grace period. Some don't but won't tell you in the bold print.

As tax time rolls around, get to an accountant to help you through your first individual tax year. Ask your professional to coach you so you can learn to do this by yourself. Be careful of any "tax expert" who also wants to help you invest your assets. Most tax professionals would never suggest such a thing, and frown on those who also sell products. You are there for one thing only—tax advice and assistance.

Always consider the tax considerations as a final parameter of managing your financial life, not the *primary* focus. The investment purpose and the optimum investment vehicle are *always* more important than *any* tax advantages or tax consequences.

Don't expect too much

Don't set up unrealistic expectations for yourself and your ability as a money manager just yet. When clinging to the side of a mountain for dear life, just hanging there is admirable. Allow yourself the mood swings you may experience. Expecting to feel and act normally or throwing yourself into your job (or compulsively enrolling in activities) may delay the healing process which is slowly working, though you may not realize it.

F-I-D-O

Forget It, Drive On is advice that you should live by. All you can do is enough, and sometimes it is over before the fat lady sings. Beating yourself about the head and shoulders for past mistakes, financial or otherwise, will not change anything. The world outside will be happy enough to do that for you, so why help?

Do you like your attitude?

People generally approach finances in one of three ways:

1. They make things happen;
2. They watch things happen for others; or
3. They wonder what's happening.

It is up to you, once you've dealt with personal issues and grieved your loss, to make things happen. Remember that luck is something that happens to prepared people. So, start preparing yourself to be more financially fit.

But don't forget: you are one human being, not a machine. Give yourself a break. Sometimes the "hurrieder" you go, the "behinder" you get. There are major changes taking place in all areas of your life. Take your time; you'll get through it.

Freud had an interesting thing to say about pain and suffering: "Avoid it whenever possible."

And if you can't, just surviving may well be victory enough for a while.

Index